J
I7
8

D0535122

OF Apr10
PLsept10
OF Nov10

Drawing in Color

Drawing in Color

Kathryn Temple

LARK BOOKS

A Division of Sterling Publishing Co., Inc.
New York / London

Editor:
JOE RHATIGAN

Art Director:
CELIA NARANJO

Photographer:
KATHRYN TEMPLE

Library of Congress Cataloging-in-Publication Data

Temple, Kathryn, 1972-
  Art for kids : drawing in color / Kathryn Temple. -- 1st ed.
       p. cm.
  Includes index.
  ISBN 978-1-57990-821-8 (hc-plc with jacket : alk. paper)
  1. Color drawing--Technique--Juvenile literature. I. Title. II. Title:
Drawing in color.
  NC758.T46 2009
  741.2--dc22
                                        2008050618

10 9 8 7 6 5 4 3 2 1

First Edition

Published by Lark Books, A Division of
Sterling Publishing Co., Inc.
387 Park Avenue South, New York, NY 10016

© 2009, Kathryn Temple

Distributed in Canada by Sterling Publishing,
c/o Canadian Manda Group, 165 Dufferin Street
Toronto, Ontario, Canada M6K 3H6

Distributed in the United Kingdom by GMC Distribution Services,
Castle Place, 166 High Street, Lewes, East Sussex, England BN7 1XU

Distributed in Australia by Capricorn Link (Australia) Pty Ltd.,
P.O. Box 704, Windsor, NSW 2756 Australia

The written instructions, photographs, designs, patterns, and projects in this volume are intended for
the personal use of the reader and may be reproduced for that purpose only. Any other use, especially
commercial use, is forbidden under law without written permission of the copyright holder.

Every effort has been made to ensure that all the information in this book is accurate. However, due
to differing conditions, tools, and individual skills, the publisher cannot be responsible for any injuries,
losses, and other damages that may result from the use of the information in this book.

If you have questions or comments about this book, please contact:
Lark Books
67 Broadway
Asheville, NC 28801
828-253-0467

Manufactured in China

All rights reserved

ISBN 13: 978-1-57990-821-8

For information about custom editions, special sales, premium and corporate purchases, please
contact Sterling Special Sales Department at 800-805-5489 or specialsales@sterlingpub.com.

Contents

FOREWORD

ONE DAY AFTER SCHOOL I SHOWED MY MOM THE COLORING BOOK PAGE I HAD WORKED SO hard on earlier that afternoon. Every color followed the rules: the tree trunk was brown, the leaves were green, and the sky was blue. I thought my mom would be really impressed.

Mom smiled and asked, "What in the world is this?" even though she knew exactly what it was. "Is this from a coloring book?" Of course that's what it is, I thought, my eyes narrowing, trying to figure what she was going to say next. She paused for a long moment and then looked at me like she was about to let me in on a big secret: "I tell you what," she said, leaning in toward me, "the next time your teacher passes out a coloring book picture, draw whatever in the world you want. A coloring book page tells you what to draw. Why don't you tell the page what you want to draw!" My heart skipped a beat when she said it. I couldn't wait to put all the whirls of color inside me down on paper.

A few days later, our teacher passed out the crayons along with a simple outline of a vase with a tulip in it. I colored in that vase and flower, but then I added roses, daisies, and flowers that existed only in my imagination. I added a door and window to the vase. I even drew a miniature person sitting underneath the shade of the blossoms as purple- and raspberry-colored petals fell all around. And do you know what happened? The teacher loved it, and my classmates became excited by the possibility of what could happen on their page!

All these years later, I've never forgotten my mom's advice. And even though I am a professional artist, I still like to break the rules. In this book, I've included all kinds of things I've learned about color and drawing over the years. There are tricks and techniques that will help you open up new worlds in your drawing. And yes, nearly every "rule" can be beautifully broken or fondly forgotten. But, the more you know, the more choices you'll have when you're making art. You can choose when to use certain rules and tools and when to toss them aside. Have fun!

Introduction

THIS BOOK COVERS MANY ASPECTS OF DRAWING, WITH A FOCUS ON COLOR. When you put a colored pencil or pastel to paper, anything is possible. All that you know, see, and imagine can appear right before your eyes. You can build a whole new wild world on a blank piece of paper.

At first, drawing some things may seem challenging, but the more you play around and the more you practice, the more you'll realize that even the most complicated subjects can be broken down into basic shapes.

The best way to use this book is to start at the beginning and work your way though it. Many of the drawing activities in these pages build on the others. In other words, to draw the bodies on page 99, it helps to have drawn the tube on page 32.

After introducing you to some drawing rules to live by and all the colorful drawing tools at your disposal, Chapter 1 will wake up your artists' eyes to an exciting world of color.

We'll cover the basics of capturing form and shape in Chapter 2: Line Drawing. If you find yourself longing to explore line drawing in greater detail, you may want to check out my first book, *Art for Kids: Drawing*.

In Chapter 3, we'll unlock the magic of light and shadow. In Chapter 4 we'll put our drawing and color skills to use by exploring still lifes. Then, in Chapter 5, we zoom out and take a look at the big picture by exploring color by drawing landscapes. Chapter 6 focuses on the magic of perspective, while in Chapter 7 you'll learn to draw your favorite animals in vivid color. Chapter 8 will help you draw the simple shapes and beautiful tones that make up the human face and body. Finally, in Chapter 9, you'll play around with everything you've learned, letting your imagination spill freely across the page.

Drawing Rules to Live By
or Life Rules to Draw By

1. There is no one right way to draw.

If you asked 100 fantastic artists to draw the same bowl of apples, you'd get 100 different drawings. You're the only artist who sees the world the way you do, and you're the only artist in the world who draws the way you do.

2. Don't compare your artwork to other people's.

If you must compare your work to anything, compare it to your own. Notice how your drawings change as you practice.

3. There's really no messing up.

If you make a mark or choose a color you're not crazy about, try to see it differently. Can you make it part of the drawing? Let your drawing change and grow as you're working on it, rather than trying to force it to look exactly a certain way. Be surprised by your accidents, instead of beating yourself up over them.

4. Practice.

If you've never drawn before, start. If you already draw, draw more. You have to be willing to make "bad" drawings in order to make good ones. Have fun with the whole process.

5. Don't stress out about showing your drawings to people.

If you want to keep all of your drawings hidden away in a portfolio or under the bed, go for it. If you want to plan an exhibition at a coffee shop or in your living room, that's great, too.

6. You're the boss.

This is your life and your artistic adventure. Follow your heart and your instincts. Trust your artistic impulses. Learn all the rules, techniques, and tricks you can, but remember: You're in charge of your art. Use the rules when you choose to and throw them out when you want.

7. Have fun!

Your Drawing Toolbox

WHEN DRAWING IN COLOR, you have lots of choices about what kind of medium, or drawing tool, you want to use. There are a number of great media for drawing in color, and they all have different qualities and are capable of producing different effects. If you have several different media in your toolbox, I encourage you to experiment with them all. If not, you can tackle most of the exercises in this book with a box of colored pencils. Remember this: You can make a great drawing out of any of the activities in this book by using whatever media you want.

Pencils/Erasers

Sometimes you'll want to start right away with color, but with some drawings, you may want to make a light pencil sketch before working with color. Invest in a good eraser—many erasers (like a lot of those cheap pink ones) leave streaks or eat up the paper.

Colored Pencils

These are great because they're vibrant and can create fine line and detail. They're also touch-sensitive, so you can get a wide range of tones from a single pencil depending upon how hard you bear down. You can also layer colored pencil to a certain extent to create new colors. Colored pencils can be used on nearly any kind of paper—thick or thin. Remember, even though they're pencils, you can't erase colored pencil markings.

Markers

Markers produce vivid, brilliant color. They create high-impact images with saturated color. They are not touch-sensitive, so, you can't vary the color by using more or less pressure. You can use markers on most kinds of paper. I like to use a paper that's not too thin and that doesn't cause my markers to bleed.

Watercolor Pencils

These are fun because they combine the magic of colored pencils and watercolors. You can draw with them just like regular colored pencils, but then you can use a wet paintbrush to dampen and blend to create washy, painterly effects. If you don't plan on using loads of water, you can use almost any kind of paper, but If you do, use a thicker, more absorbent paper.

Oil Pastels

Oil pastels have rich color and a nice thick texture. Unlike some of the other media, oil pastels actually have some *body*. If you run your finger over an oil pastel drawing, you can feel the marks on the page. You can layer oil pastel to a certain extent. So, if you don't quite like the color of something, you can work right on top of it with another color. Use a paper that has some texture, or *tooth*, to it.

Pastels

Pastels are fun because they blend and smudge. They're great for drawings where you want soft edges. You want to store these drawings with great care because it's easy to accidentally smear a pastel artwork. Use a thicker paper with texture on its surface. Since pastels are so dusty, they need the tooth of the paper to hold onto the pigment and keep it there.

Watercolor Paints

Watercolors are beautiful because they create transparent washes of color. Once you put a mark down in watercolor, you can't take it back. This is great because it teaches you to work with what you've got and to incorporate any "mistakes" into your drawing rather than trying to hide them. With watercolors, you need to use a thick watercolor paper that can act like a sponge and absorb all of that water. When choosing brushes, use the synthetic bristle watercolor brushes that have a "Filbert" shape. Get a couple of good brushes, a small one and a large one, and take really good care of them by washing thoroughly after each use.

Paper

When you go to the art store, or even the art supply section of a craft store, you'll find there are different papers to choose from. They differ in a number of ways, but the two major factors are thickness and texture. Another way artists talk about paper thickness is in terms of heaviness or how many *pounds* it is. A 240-lb. paper, for example, is going to be a lot thicker than an 80-lb. paper. The artsy way to talk about paper surface texture is to talk about its tooth. When you're drawing with dusty materials like pastel, you want a paper with enough of a rough surface or tooth to hold onto the pigment.

Keep plenty of paper on hand. When you have lots of paper, you're going to feel freer to take creative risks and give yourself the room to play and experiment.

OPEN YOUR EYES TO COLOR

MOST PEOPLE THINK THAT THE MAGIC of a beautiful drawing lies in the skill and precision of the artist's hand—like some people are born with a special ability that most people don't have. Don't believe it for a second! Everyone can draw, and the trick isn't about who can draw the steadiest line. The truth is, the secret isn't in the artist's hand at all. It's in his or her eyes.

Drawing is really about how you see the world and how you interpret the information your eyes receive. This type of seeing goes beyond the regular seeing you're doing right now. It's like putting on a pair of mysterious glasses and suddenly noticing the flecks of yellow in your brother's eyes or how the water glass reflects the red and yellow of the magazine it's sitting on top of.

When you open your artist's eyes, you're looking at things with a curiosity and an attention most people rarely use. You'll notice that something you once used to describe simply as "red" actually has a range of colors in it, from dark blues to oranges! You'll start to see that there are a zillion different reds and blues and yellows and greens and purples and oranges. You'll spy colors you don't even have names for yet!

Develop Your Artist's Eyes

We all have artist's eyes, but not all of us know how to use them. Here are some quick ways to fine-tune yours:

- Daydream
- Space out
- Stare at stuff
- Stare out the window
- Squint your eyes and see what colors jump out at you
- Slow down

Once you begin to see the nuance of color—the hues, shadows, and gradations—you can begin to use them in your drawings.

Brain Games

When you're reading a book or doing homework, you're using the part of your brain that reasons and recognizes symbols (usually the left side of your brain). Most adults and a lot of kids use this part of their brain most of the time. The trouble is, if you try to draw from this part of your brain, you'll draw your idea or symbol of what you're looking at, rather than actually seeing what you're looking at. So, if you're drawing an apple, your reasoning brain will say, "I've got this symbol for an apple that looks like this."

Your creative, artist's brain doesn't get a chance to have fun and see all of the unique curves and shapes of the specific apple you're looking at. Likewise, your reasoning brain will step in and say that the apple is red, and it will tell you to color your little apple symbol in a flat red color. Your artist's brain gets cheated out of all the fun of seeing the range of colors in that beautiful apple that make it look good enough to eat.

Instead of this,

you can draw this!

This book is all about exercising the creative part of your brain!

Color Wheels

When someone asks you what your favorite color is, what colors flash through your mind? Most people consider six or eight basic colors when deciding their answer to that age-old question. But take a minute to look around the room where you are right now. How many different colors and shades of colors do you see? Do you see colors you don't even really have a name for? There are more than a hundred, or a thousand, or even a million colors. Like stars in the galaxy, there are nearly limitless colors to be discovered in our world! Color wheels are tools that help us organize colors and understand how they relate to one another.

There are three colors that are different from all the rest: red, yellow, and blue. They are called *primary colors* and, without them, you wouldn't have any of the others. They can be mixed in different combinations to make millions of other colors.

When you mix red and yellow, you make orange. Yellow and blue create green. If you mix blue and red, you get purple. Orange, green, and purple are called the secondary colors.

the primary colors

color wheel with primary & secondary colors

If you want to take this a step further, you can mix a little bit of each secondary color with the primary color next to it on the color wheel. So, when you mix green and yellow, you get a lighter, yellowish green that we can call yellow-green. If you mix green and blue, you'll get a darker, bluer green that we can call blue-green. You could continue this process of mixing a little bit of two colors that are side-by-side on the color wheel until you had hundreds and hundreds of different colors.

You can make even more colors by adding white to your color. If you add white to red, you'll get pink. If you add white to green, you'll get a lighter green. But this light green will be different from the lighter green you got when you mixed yellow-green. It will be icier, a little cooler, less warm and yellow. We'll tackle mixing colors with your different media on page 21.

Spend some time with your different media creating and playing with the color wheel. Note the colors you really like and want to use.

color wheel with primary,
secondary & tertiary colors

Cool & Warm Colors

You'll often hear artists talking about warm and cool colors. This is a way of talking about how colors behave in a picture and how they make you feel when you look at them.

Blues, greens, grays, and some purples are considered to be cool colors. Think of a cool spring breeze through the shimmering green leaves of a tree. Imagine the clear blue water in a swimming pool or a wintry landscape, with the tall trunks of trees casting bluish purple shadows across the snow. Cool colors are soothing. They don't smack you in the eye when you look at a picture, but instead seem happy to just hang out and wait for you to notice them.

Chapter 1: Open Your Eyes to Color

Reds, oranges, yellows, and some browns are warm colors. These tend to pop out at you. Imagine your friend's red cheeks when you're running around outside. Have you ever looked out the window of the car and noticed red flowers growing in the middle of all of those cool colors? They stand right out and demand that you notice them.

Of course, there are no absolute rules about warm and cool colors. Colors are utterly magical and can do whatever they want. You can create a drawing where a cool color jumps right off the page or where a warm color looks like it's miles away. Once you understand how colors interact with one another, you can make them break all kinds of rules. Also, once you see the difference between warm and cool colors, you'll find that it gets even trickier. If you look at two shades of blue, you might notice that one is a little warmer than the other. There are warm grays and cool grays, warm reds and cool reds, etc.

How Colors Relate

Do you act differently when you're at your grandmother's house than you do when you're at the park with your best friend? You're still the same essential person, but different aspects of your personality come out depending upon your company and environment. Same goes for color.

Which color on the left matches the yellow in the center of the blue square?

Did you pick the bright yellow on the far left? It's hard to believe that the bright, canary yellow inside the blue rectangle actually matches the dark, yellow ocher color second to the left. The cool blue brings out all of the bright, sunny characteristics of this yellow's personality. But, when you put that same yellow in between a lighter, lemony yellow and a brighter, warmer yellow, it showcases all of the browner elements of the same color.

Complements

The colors that are directly across from each other on the color wheel have a very special relationship. They're called *complementary colors* or complements. They are the exact opposite of one another. So, when you put them next to one another, they zing. They have amazing contrast and create a lot of energy when they're side-by-side. They're like best friends who are total opposites, and yet bring out the best in each other.

Do you notice anything about the temperature of complementary pairs? (One is cool and one is warm!)

Check out these pairs of complements.

However, if you mix complementary colors (by adding a bit of each color of paint, or by overlapping colored pencil lines), you'll find that the effect is completely different—they mellow each other and you get different neutral, brownish colors. Though these colors are more toned down than the originals, they can be beautiful, important colors in your drawings.

After Image

Stare at the little black dot in the middle of this orange circle and count slowly to 20. When you've finished counting, stare at the black dot on the blank white part of this page. Do you see a glowing circular shape? What color is it? Blue?! Blue is the complementary color of orange. Try this in your sketchbook with other colors on the color wheel. Even without your help, your eyeballs recognize complementary colors! If they get tired of seeing one color, in this case orange, they start leaning the opposite direction and see blue!

Complements Create Contrast

Notice how these weird cool creatures create a kind of visual harmony but nothing really jumps out too much to grab your attention.

You get the same harmonious effect with a group of warm color creatures.

Which bouquet do you notice first? Even though the flowers are only a tiny part of the whole picture, the orange ones really stand out for a couple of reasons. First, they are a warm color against a cool background, creating a strong contrast. Second, the orange flowers are the complementary color of blue.

See how it works the same way in reverse. The blue bouquet stands out the most in the group of warm creatures.

Mix 'em Up

There are different ways to make new colors depending on the kind of medium you're using. If you're painting and you want to make a darker, bluer green, you simply add a little bit of blue paint to the green paint until you have the color you want. With colored pencils and other dry media, you can overlap colors, or mix marks of different colors to get a new color.

Try This

Think about the color wheel and pick two colored pencils that are primary colors. Play around with layering them to make a secondary color. See these three oranges on the right? For each I drew a patch of yellow and then added red over it. Each time I pressed down a little harder to get a different intensity.

Now Try This

Pick a red, blue, yellow, and white colored pencil, and experiment with overlapping these colors in different combinations. See how many different colors you can make. Try drawing light, soft layers of color to make lighter shades. Then try layering harder, thicker layers of color. I created all of these colors by mixing red, blue, yellow, and white.

Which Green Is Darker?

Most people will say the green rectangle on the right is darker. Guess what? They're the same exact color green. How can this be? The green rectangle on the left is broken up with white stripes. The one on the right is broken up by black stripes. The eye mixes these colors when you look at the green. In other words, the eye mixes the green on the left with white, giving us the illusion that it's a lighter shade of green. And it also mixes the green on the right with black, giving us the illusion that it's a darker shade of green.

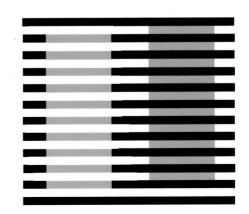

More Mixing

What does all this mixing have to do with drawing? First, it reminds us how colors are not fixed and static but instead are relative. They change and shift in relation to their surroundings. Second, it shows us that we can make a color lighter or darker by mixing it with a lighter or darker color. It also shows us that we can mix a color with the color of our paper.

If you're drawing on a white page and want a lighter green, you can leave bits of white between your green marks—your eye will mix the green and white together to make a lighter green!

Or, if you want a yellowier green, try mixing in some yellow lines with the green lines. When you draw with these straight little parallel lines it's called "hatching."

If you criss-cross your hatch-marks like this it's called "cross hatching."

These techniques work really well with other media such as markers, which are virtually unmixable.

What About Complements?

Like I said on page 19, when complements are side-by-side they intensify each other—they make each other pop. But, when you mix them together, the opposite happens—they tone each other down.

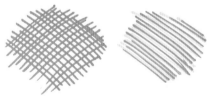

See how adding blue makes this orange more brown and mellow?

See how adding orange makes this blue darker and a little duller?

Connecting with Color

While it's important to understand the theory of how colors work, it's just as important to tap into how we feel about different colors and how different colors make us feel. We all have favorite colors and different associations with colors. Just for a moment, let go of all of your ideas about making a drawing that "looks like" something. Instead, let loose and explore color as freely as you may have when you were a tiny little kid playing with crayons for the first time.

Emotions

Using the medium of your choice, draw different emotions such as joy, excitement, sadness, or fear. Resist the urge to draw a smiley face, or some other representation for joy. Instead, use only abstract marks and shapes and blobs of color. Let the color itself and the way you make your marks on the paper communicate the feeling. While you're drawing each emotion, commit to it completely. Try to feel it as you're drawing it. Let your hand and arm move across the page in a way that embodies the feeling.

Here's my drawing of fear.

Musical Colors

Turn on a song that you like or that inspires you. Draw along to the music. What color does that note sound like? How do your shapes and marks respond to the rhythm of the piece?

Can you match the drawings to the music that inspired them?
One is punk and the other is classical.

LINE DRAWING

BEFORE WE GET TOO FAR INTO THE WORLD of color, it's important to talk about line drawing for a moment. It's sort of like this: before painting your fabulous new tree house, you first have to build the structure, construct the walls, and hammer the floorboards into place. Line drawing is how we build the structure of the object we're drawing. It's how we find the form, the shape of the things we want to bring to life on the page.

Drawing is like learning a new language; you're figuring out how to translate the world you see into simple lines and shapes on your paper. Fortunately, drawing isn't a language that requires you to learn 100,000 new words. You can break down everything you see into simple lines and shapes. When you look around at all of the possibilities—all of the different things you might want to draw such as people, buildings, frogs, flowers—it's thrilling to find that all of these complicated forms can be drawn with basic lines and shapes!

Draw with a regular graphite pencil when you're searching for the shapes that will make up your drawing. Since you know you can always erase and move things around, you'll be more relaxed and free while exploring with line. As you move along, you may want to forget about the pencil altogether and dive right in with whatever colorful tools you have: markers, colored pencils, pastels, watercolors, whatever!

Draw a Vase

START WITH SOMETHING SIMPLE. Vases are great objects to draw because of their elegant lines and simple construction.

Step 1
Draw ellipses for the mouth, body, and base of the vase.

Step 2
Sketch the neck of the vase by connecting the top ellipse with the fatter, rounder ellipse with a curved, parenthesis-type line on each side. Use a curved line to connect the bottom of the fat ellipse with the base ellipse on both sides. Draw a round line for the inside lip of the vase.

Step 3
Erase any parts of the guideline ellipses that fall "inside" the vase. Draw it again and again.

On Your Own

Find a vase (or a pitcher or mug if you can't find a vase) and set it in front of you. Spend a few minutes looking at the object. How big is its mouth in relation to the base? Is it taller than it is wide? What is its widest part? Notice that in the example I drew a fatter, rounder ellipse for the center of the vase. What does yours look like?

Draw Stuff!

TAKE A LOOK AT THESE OBJECTS. Do you see how you can use your artist's eyes to find the shapes within them? Practice looking for the simple shapes in the things around you. Find objects around your house and practice drawing them. Whenever something seems too complex, try to simplify it down to its most basic shapes.

Drawing Apples

HERE'S YOUR CHANCE TO DRAW AN APPLE like the one on page 13 (the one on the right!). Find an apple and place it on a table about a foot or two from where you'll be sitting. Remember, you don't have to "nail" the shape in one sweeping stroke of the pencil. Feel free to sketch around your shape several times, changing it to your liking each time until you have the shape you want. When I'm drawing, I often have several overlapping light lines in my sketch and I'll pick the one I like the most and start to define it by darkening that line.

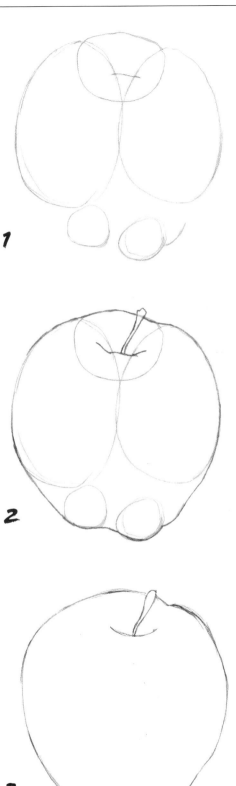

Step 1
Observe the apple closely and notice where it bulges and curves. (Most apples are far from perfectly round.) Draw ellipses for each major lump you see in the top of the apple. Next, draw smaller, rounder shapes for the little lumps at the bottom of the apple. I don't always draw the full ellipse, but instead just make a curved line here and there.

Step 2
Use smooth, curved lines to connect your bulges and define the overall shape of the apple. Pay special attention to the little indentation where the apple stem grows.

Step 3
Erase any parts of the guideline ellipses that fall inside the apple outline.

Drawing Tiger

MY 13-YEAR-OLD NEIGHBOR, JANIKA, ADOPTED TIGER when she started hanging out around her house. Tiger adores being pet and cuddled so much that she can defy the force of gravity and jump all the way up into your arms even if you're standing up.

Step 1
Look at the kitten and notice how her body is shaped. Where are the biggest sections of her body? What shapes are they? Draw the ovals for the head, body, and butt.

Step 2
Draw the ovals for the cat's left thigh and the four paws.

Step 3
Take a moment to look at the kitten and notice the curves of its legs and the lines that connect the paw circles to the body. Which lines bulge outward and which curve inward? Sketch these curved lines of the legs. Look at the funny shape of the tale. It's a little bit triangular and a little bit tube-like.

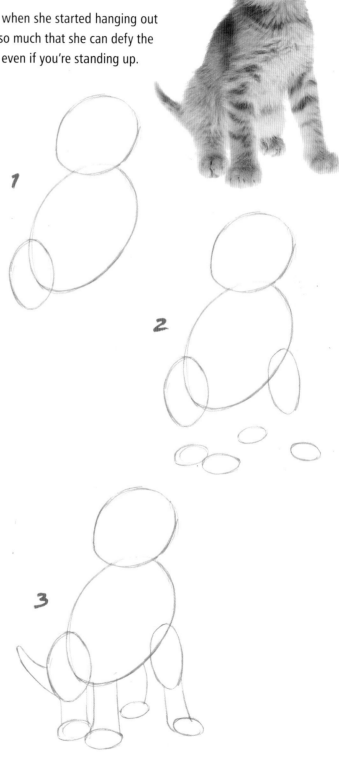

Step 4

Draw the triangular shapes for the ears. Draw small ovals for the eyes and nose. For the kitten's little muzzle, draw two ovals side by side that touch or almost touch. For the chin, draw a little circle right underneath these two ovals, snug up against them. Draw the two tiny lines of the neck, connecting the head oval with the body oval.

Step 5

Clean up your drawing a little bit. Use your pencil to emphasize the lines that you like and erase a lot of your guidelines and internal shapes. Notice that your cat isn't finished. The idea here is to get the shape of the kitten to your liking. You're getting ready to add color, which you'll do on page 82.

On Your Own

Unless your kitten is sleeping, she probably won't sit for a portrait for very long. If you want to do a detailed drawing like this one, try working from a photograph. If you want to practice capturing movement and basic shapes, try sketching lots of little kittens on your page—a new one every time she moves.

Chapter 3

LIGHT, SHADOW & COLOR

ONE OF THE MOST IMPORTANT THINGS in drawing is learning to see how light falls over an object—how it illuminates some areas, casts shadows over others, and affects the colors we see. Light and shadow give our drawings a sense of dimension and presence—like there's something on that page with weight and substance that you can actually reach in and touch.

The first thing you need to do when drawing is identify the direction of your light source. Where is the light coming from? Is it coming from a big, general source that sheds light evenly over everything—like the noonday sun outside, or an overhead light in a room? Or is it coming from a more specific direction—like light streaming through a window into a dim room, casting long shadows across the floor?

Take a look at the mug below. Do you see the dark shadow cast on the table? Look at the right side of the mug. Do you see how the colors are lighter? Do you see the brightest, white, highlight area on the mug? Can you identify the direction of the light source? Here's a hint: the things farther away from the light source will be darker, while the things closer to it will be lighter.

Notice that even though the mug is light green it also has dark green, yellow, white, and even tiny specks of light blue in it. Once you can see the shapes made by the light and shadow areas, you'll start noticing them on all kinds of objects.

Value Scales

When we talk about the value of a color, we're talking about how dark or light it is. The shadowy shapes in the green mug are simply blocks of color of different values. The colored strips below are *value scales*, and they're useful tools when learning how to create the different values that make drawings come alive.

Each block in a value scale contains a different value, ranging from the lightest to the darkest. Create your own scales and practice making each block an even *step* in value. The more you practice the better you'll be able to identify and draw the values that you see. How do you create darker and lighter values? It depends on the medium you're using.

Colored Pencils: You control the value by how hard or soft you bear down on your pencil.

Pastels: Crayon and pastel also respond to pressure.

Watercolors: You control the value of your paint by adding more or less water.

Markers: Try *stippling*, which is making lots of little dots. You can also try hatching and cross-hatching (see page 22).

Oil Pastels: These are pressure-sensitive to a certain extent, but you can also get good effects by using colors of different value and layering them.

The Blue Tube

Tools Used: Colored Pencils

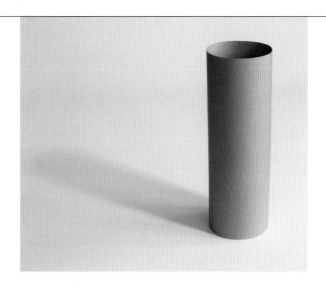

YOU CAN START WITH a regular pencil if you wish, but since this is a relatively simple shape, I went straight for the colored pencils. You may think it strange to be drawing a tube, but they're everywhere! You can find them in vases, bicycles, spaceships, even in people. So, learning to draw a tube will actually come in handy. For this activity, you can use a toilet-paper tube, or, if you want something more colorful, you can roll a piece of paper and tape it in the back. That's what I did to make my blue tube. Then, you'll want to set it on a table with a strong light source next to it (such as a lamp). Turn off any overhead lights so the shadows are dramatic and easier to see.

Step 1
With a medium blue pencil, draw two ellipses for the top and bottom openings of the tube. Next draw two straight lines connecting them.

Step 2
Use the same medium blue to draw a shadow along the left side of the tube. Draw the shadow on the inside lip of the tube on the right side. This is sort of a backward "C" shape. The light source in this photo is on the right, so the darkest shadows are on the left side, farthest away from the light source.

Step 3
Draw the lighter blue shadow on the middle left side of the tube. You can use the same colored pencil as before, simply don't bear down as hard. Also draw the middle values inside the tube.

Step 4

Draw the lightest blue tones on the right side of the tube and the left part of the inside lip. These are the areas of the tube that are getting the most light. Bearing down harder, darken the dark areas, creating more of a sense of volume.

Step 5

Using an even darker blue, color the darkest shadow areas even further.

Step 6

Use a gray pencil to draw a long, diagonal shadow behind the tube.

Step 7

Bearing down harder with the grey pencil, draw the darker two triangular sections of the cast shadow. Do you see any unexpected shapes in your cast shadow? The triangular shapes in this image indicate that, even though I had one strong light source, there are other light sources in the room. Notice how the darkest gray is closest to where the tube sits on the table, where there's going to be the least light.

On Your Own

Look around your house for tube-shaped objects to draw. Can you find a candlestick, lamp, or bottle that has a tube as its primary shape? Draw them! Next, use your imagination to make something new with a tube shape. What if you give the tube a pointed tip and add a couple of triangular shapes to the base? Can you draw a space shuttle?

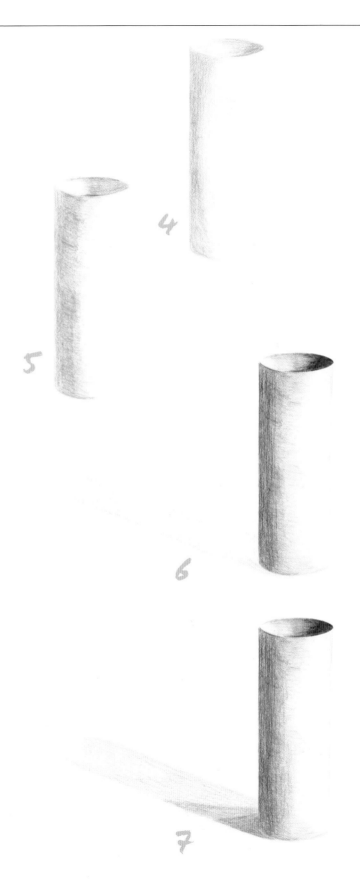

Drawing Spheres

Tools Used: Oil Pastels, Colored Paper

OIL PASTELS ARE COOL because you can color right on top of what you've already drawn to lighten or darken the area. Place an orange on the table a foot or two in front of your drawing paper. Adjust a lamp (preferably one of those with a bendy neck) so that it shines down above the orange from one side or the other. I like to cast long shadows.

Step 1

Notice where the light source is coming from. With a yellow-orange pastel, sketch the basic shape of the orange. Don't worry about making it perfect—just sketch around the circle a few times until you find a shape you like. Sketch in the part of the orange that's the yellow-orange color.

Step 2

With a medium or red-orange color, sketch in the middle part of the orange. This is the part of the orange that isn't in dark shadow but also isn't the most brightly lit.

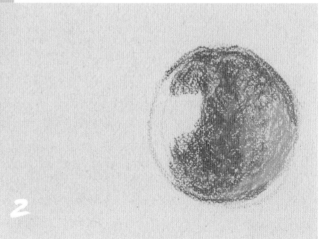

Step 3

With a brownish-orange pastel, sketch in the darker shadow area of the orange. This is a very small area of the orange, but it's very important in making the drawing look round.

Step 4

Use a medium orange color to fill in any little flecks of paper that are showing. Pressing down pretty hard, draw in little circular motions and overlap the yellow-orange and brownish areas a little bit so they blend. Go over some of the light areas with a yellow-orange color.

Step 5

Finally, draw the shadow on the table, and use your white pastel to add a bright, crisp highlight to the right side of the orange. Use a lighter and darker gray for the shadow. The darkest part of the shadow is closest to the orange, right underneath its curve where it sits on the table. It's like a cave. The deeper you walk into it, the less light there is and the darker it gets.

On Your Own

Look around for other sphere-shaped objects to draw. Try to find more complicated shapes that are composed of spheres. Use what you know about how light falls over individual round objects to draw a luscious bunch of grapes!

Notice how light bounces off the table and makes a highlight where you'd least expect it!

Drawing Eggs

Tools Used: Pencil, Eraser, Watercolor Paints, Paintbrush

WITH WATERCOLOR, IT'S IMPORTANT TO REMEMBER THAT YOU CAN ALWAYS GO DARKER, but it's next to impossible to lighten things up once the paint has soaked into the paper. When I draw an egg, I like to set it on the table in front of me. In order to prevent a messy, humpty-dumpty disaster, either put a loop of tape (sticky side out) underneath the egg to hold it to the table, or sprinkle a little pile of salt on the table and rest your egg on top of it. Set up a lamp on one side of the egg so that you've got a strong light source. This will make it easier to see the lights and shadows and to make the egg look round.

Step 1
Lightly draw the shape of the egg with the pencil. Remember you don't have to get it right the first time. Once you're happy with the shape, lighten your final pencil mark with the eraser. Since this egg is brown, lightly paint it with a reddish-brown watercolor.

Step 2
Look for the shadows on the egg. When you squint and look at your egg, where are the darkest areas? Use your watered-down reddish brown color to paint the right side of the egg in shadow. (Can you see how my brush strokes followed the curve of the egg? Instead of up and down marks, I painted curved lines, sort of like backward letter C's.)

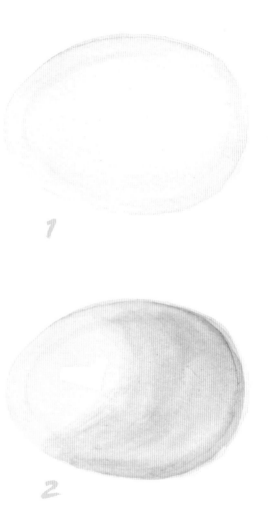

Step 3

Mix your reddish-brown with a little bit of a darker, cooler brown, and add darker shadows to the far right side of the egg. The darker, cooler brown makes this part of the egg move back into the space and gives the whole egg more of a sense of volume.

Step 4

Take a moment to notice the shadow that's cast on the table as the light spills over the egg. Use dark gray to paint the wide elliptical shadow to the right of the egg. Notice how the darkest part of the shadow is closest to the egg.

On Your Own

Practice drawing your egg from different angles. How does the shape change?

Ferris Wheel

Tools Used: Pencil, Eraser, Markers

KEEP YOUR EYE OUT FOR COOL THINGS to draw. Anything that catches your eye can be used for drawing practice. Here's a fun object I drew at a state fair. Give it a try.

Step 1

Take a moment to look at the Ferris wheel. Notice how the big oval shapes tilt a little to the right. Draw a big oval. Keep your arm loose and let your hand circle around and around on the page until you have a shape you like. Then, sketch the ellipse for the back ring of the wheel. Draw the circles in the middle where all of the spokes attach, and draw the big steel legs on the front and the back.

Step 2

Sketch the straight lines that represent the spokes that hold the Ferris wheel together. Start by drawing the spokes on the front oval.

Step 3

Draw the lines for the spokes of the back oval. Notice how they're just off to the right from the ones in front.

Step 4

Now that you have a good structure to hang the buggies on, begin sketching in the ovals for the carriages. This Ferris wheel has little round buggies with an umbrella over each one.

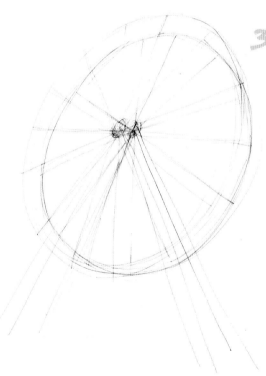

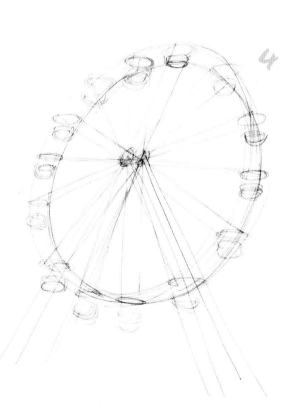

Step 5

Go in a little darker with your pencil and start shaping things up. Add definition to the buggies. Darken the top edge of each buggy, and then add the little straight lines that connect each buggy to its umbrella.

Step 6

Start to add color. You can either match the colors or use whatever colors you like! First, quickly block in the colors for the buggies and the big, steel beams. With most markers you can almost always make a color darker, but you can't lighten it up once you've drawn something. So, start with the lightest colors you have. Leave some white space on some of the buggies. This is where the highlights will be. See how I used a bright turquoise blue for the front legs and greyer green for the back legs? Remember that bright colors jump forward and grayer colors tend to recede, or move back.

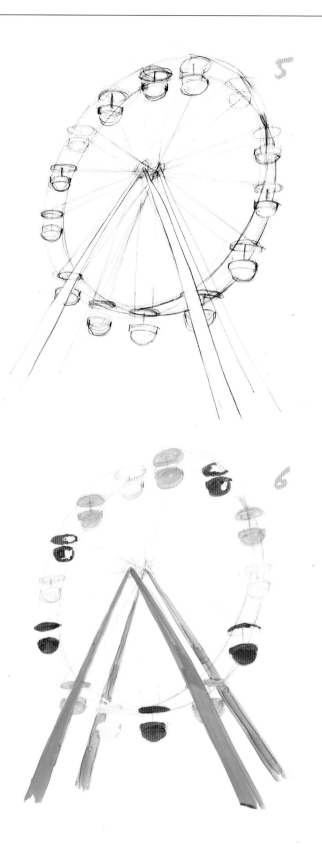

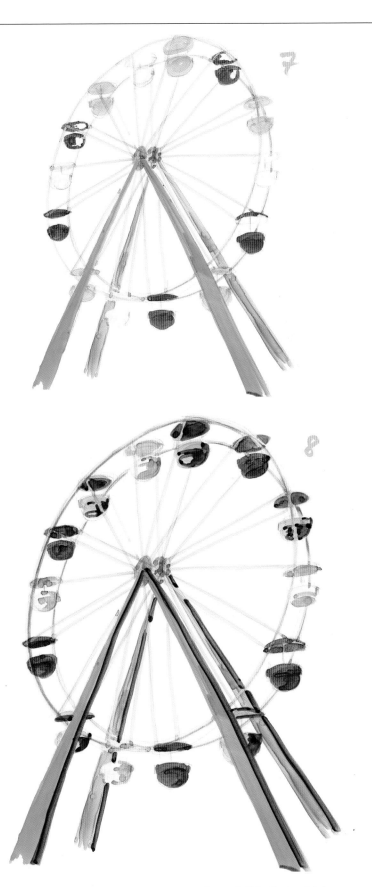

Step 7
Add color to the spokes and the oval shaped frame.

Step 8
The brightest light is coming from the left side of the picture. So, the darker shadows will be on the right sides and bottoms of the buggies. Take a look at the big oval that's closest to you. See how the inside lip of the left side has a dark shadow on it? Go ahead and draw this shadow. Darken some of the shadow areas a little bit more. Add the lines that connect each buggy to its umbrella. Darken the front spokes a bit. I used a gray colored pencil for the detail of the criss-crossed support bars between the spokes.

On Your Own

Try drawing *en plein air*. This is French for, "in the open air." There are a lot of famous artists you've probably heard of who drew and painted this way. Van Gogh and Monet both made astonishingly beautiful artwork by taking their easels and paints outside and observing the world. So, pack up your sketchbook and your pastels or colored pencils and head outside to draw!

Drawing Fabric

You finally have a good, artistic excuse not to make up your bed! Drawing a rumpled-up sheet is one of the best ways to practice seeing lights and shadows. Where the fabric folds or twists or buckles up, the sheet will make different shapes. These are wacky abstract forms—not like the ellipses and circles in a vase or a cat. So, have patience with yourself and draw what you see. If you're having trouble, zoom in and draw a smaller section.

Step 1
Sketch the lines of the folds of fabric with a light blue pencil. If you have a hard time seeing these lines, squint.

1

Step 2

Go back in with the same pencil and start building up the shadow areas. For the darker shadows, bear down harder.

Step 3

Use a darker, medium blue to define the shadow areas even further.

Step 4

With a light blue pencil, lightly sketch over the entire cloth area to fill in most of the white. I only left a few small areas of white where I saw highlights on the sheet.

Step 5

Go back in with the light and medium blues to deepen the color of some of the folds. Finally, use a dark bluish-green color to intensify the darkest shadows.

On Your Own

Take the art of the messy bed to a whole new level. Rather than letting the composition be accidental, spend a moment arranging the sheet so that the shapes of the wrinkles and shadows aren't so complex. Arrange the fabric into fewer, simpler shapes. You can also arrange a piece of fabric or cloth napkin in front of you on a table.

Chapter 4

STILL LIFE DRAWING

A STILL LIFE IS A LITTLE ARRANGEMENT OF OBJECTS that you set up to draw. It's fun because you can choose whatever objects you want and arrange them however you like. Use really traditional still life objects such as fruit or vases, or more personal items such as your sneaker, a favorite toy, or a wadded-up piece of chewing gum. You can make a group of plastic toy frogs wait in line to jump in a mug. Or, arrange a traditional object, such as an apple, in an unexpected way. You're really only limited by your imagination.

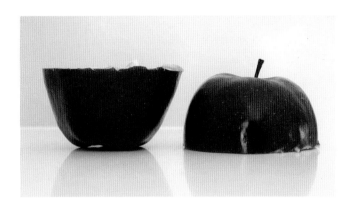

red in the bottom left corner to balance things out. If your composition seems overly cluttered, remove one or two things until you like the way it looks. Finally, pay attention to the light in your still life. Do you want to have one, main, strong light source? If so, you may want to set a lamp up right next to one side of your still life. Or, you could place your still life on a table next to a bright, sunny window. Then, turn off the overhead light so it doesn't compete with your other light source. Having one, strong directional light source adds drama to your still life by making it have higher contrast (darker darks and lighter lights) and by keeping most of your bright, highlight areas on one side and most of your shadow areas on the other.

To set up a still life, select your objects and arrange them on the table in front of you. You might want to start simply with a single object on a simple surface. As you continue drawing, you may want to add more objects to your compositions. Take your time situating the various objects into a composition that you like. If you take a step back and think something is missing, add an object. Maybe your still life needs a touch of

Simple Still Life

Tools Used: Pencil, Eraser, Colored Pencils

FOR THIS STILL LIFE, I chose a bright, juicy red delicious apple. I used a high wattage clamp lamp to light it from the right side.

Step 1
After drawing a plump apple shape in pencil (see page 27), use your eraser to lighten the pencil marks. Choose a bright, warm red colored pencil. Look at the set-up. Where is the main light source? Where are the highlights? Squint to see the big areas of this warm, red color. Go ahead and color in this area. Leave the other areas white for now. It's especially important to make sure the highlight area stays white.

Step 2
Select a darker, cooler red for your shadow areas. Look for the darkest shadows on the apple. On the apple in the photograph, the darkest shadow areas are on the left side of the apple and on both sides of the stem. You can tell from the shadows cast by the apple stem that, even though my strongest light source was to the right, there were other light sources in the room.

Step 3

The apple in the photograph has a dark-yellow ocher color in the stem indentation. Use a dark brown and a lighter, reddish-brown for the stem. Notice how both sides of the stem are dark and that there's a highlight in the center. Use the warm red pencil (from step 1) to go back over some of the bright red areas. Then shape the highlight and make it a little more speckled. Once you've completed this step, you'll see your apple really start to take shape.

3

Step 4

Use a cool, dark red to darken some of the shadows and to add a little definition to the right edge of the apple. Again, use the warm red to blend the areas between colors and to deepen the warm reds of the apple skin. Use light and dark gray pencils to cast the shadow. Notice how the darkest areas are just underneath the apple where it sits on the table.

On Your Own

Try drawing a bright green Granny Smith apple. Or, take a big bite out of an apple and draw it! Also, play with lighting situations so you can practice noticing shadows.

4

Complicated Still Life

Tools Used: Pencil, Eraser, Oil Pastels

DO THE ELEMENTS IN THIS PHOTOGRAPH look familiar? For this still life, I arranged the vase from page 25 on the crumpled sheet from page 42. Once I added a tulip, the scene started to shape up into a nice little composition. You can continue to add objects until you have an arrangement you're happy with.

Step 1
Sketch the vase and the fabric, and then draw the tulip. Go over the drawing lightly with your eraser to soften the pencil lines.

1

Step 2

Use a yellow-ocher color for the ellipse at the mouth, and a medium green for the shadow areas. Bear down harder for the darker areas. Use a moss green for the shadows on the leaves and stem.

2

3

Step 3

Use light blue to outline the fabric. Keep your line really relaxed and quickly block in the color with loose, easy marks.

Step 4

Use a warm red for some of the tulip petals, leaving the shadow areas white. Use a light green for the lighter areas of the leaves and stem. On the highlighted area of the vase, use the yellow-ocher color. (I used this color because I didn't have a pastel that matched the warm yellowish-green color of the vase. I could have just used a different one, but I thought it would be fun to try mixing it with the pastels.) You can overlap and smudge oil pastels quite a bit, so you can experiment with making different colors.

4

5

Step 5

Use a slightly darker blue to deepen the shadows on the fabric. Use brown for the shadow area inside the neck of the vase and light green to smudge and overlap the yellow-ocher area of the vase. You can also use the light green in the transition area between the yellow-ocher and the dark green shadow.

Step 6

Use a darker, cool red for the shadowy bottom of the tulip and a dark purple for the shadow of the inside the petals. Use a dark green to make the shadow on the vase more dramatic. I colored the background a grayish lavender. Oops! I forgot to leave the whole highlight area white! Luckily, oil pastels layer pretty well, so I used some white to emphasize the highlight.

Step 7

I took a look at the whole composition and didn't like the way it looked. I felt like it needed more contrast, a bit more zip. So I changed the back-ground color to a much richer blue. Much better. Always feel free to follow your instincts!

6

7

On Your Own

You just drew a really traditional still life. It's made up of the kind of classical elements you'd find in an old masterpiece. Now, go find some of your favorite zany objects and create a modern, funky still life. Or use really "boring" and "unartistic" things such as a dirty gym sock or a crumpled up gum wrapper, and see how you can breathe new life into them.

Chapter 5

DRAWING IN PERSPECTIVE

THIS CHAPTER FOCUSES ON USING color and perspective techniques to create drawings that feel remarkably three-dimensional.

With a few lines you can draw miles of railroad track, a convincing box, a building, or even library shelves. Linear perspective rules help us understand the way that things with straight edges behave in space. See how the railroad track looks like it stretches for miles? As it moves away from us, the edges appear to get closer together, until they finally touch, deep in the distance.

If we understand how the illusion works, then we can translate these sorts of objects onto paper. See how all of the parallel lines of the library shelves appear to be getting closer together as they move into the distance? The imaginary point that they point toward (as in the library shelves) or eventually touch (as in the railroad tracks) is called the *vanishing point*. This point rests on the horizon line, which you can see clearly in the photo of the train tracks. Indoors and in other more cluttered landscape shots, you have to imagine the horizon line in the distance, back behind what you're drawing. These two photographs demonstrate the concept called *one-point perspective*.

Now, take a look at this glass building. See how it also has parallel lines moving into the distance? Do you see the difference between it and the railroad tracks? Instead of just having one vanishing point, it has two. This is called *two-point perspective*.

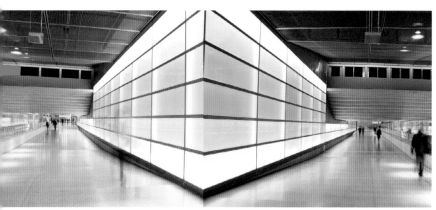

One-Point Perspective (Outside of a Box)

Tools Used: Pencil, Eraser, Colored Pencils, Ruler

DRAWING A CUBE USING ONE-POINT PERSPECTIVE is the first step to drawing all kinds of things, including chairs, tables, steps, houses, buildings, books, and more. And when you add what you know about color and shading, you can make all kinds of fabulous three-dimensional stuff!

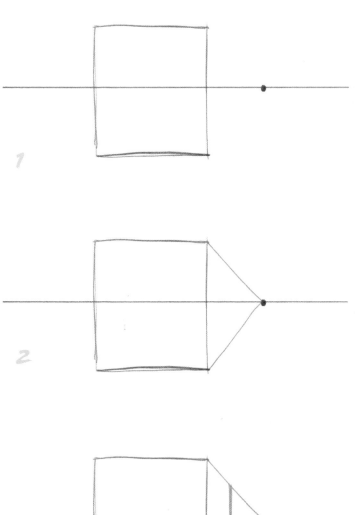

Step 1
Draw a horizon line across your page. Draw a square somewhere along this line. (Later you can experiment with what happens when you put your cube above or below the horizon line.) Next, draw a dot somewhere on your horizon line. This is going to be your vanishing point.

Step 2
Draw lines connecting the top and bottom corners closest to the vanishing point.

Step 3
Draw the back edge of the cube. This line should be straight up and down, like the right and left sides of the cube.

Step 4

Erase the back two perspective lines that connect the box to the vanishing point. Erase the bit of the horizon line that is inside the cube. Now you have a cool cube drawn in perspective.

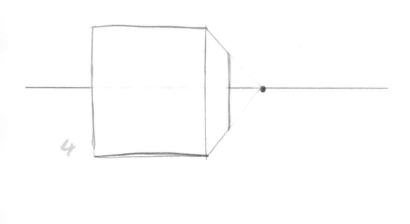

Step 5

Imagine the light source coming from the left side of the drawing. Color the front square of the cube a light, warm orange. Next, color the right side of the cube a darker orange. You can choose different colors, but you'll want the warm, light color closer to your light source and the darker color farther away.

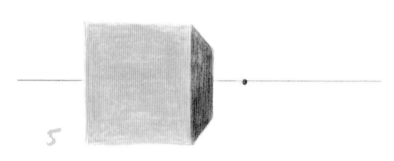

Step 6

Choose a dark, cool color to draw the cast shadow to the side of the cube. Use a lighter hue of the same color for the ground.

On Your Own

Try this again but start with a rectangle instead of a square. How does that change your finished box? Experiment by making boxes of all different lengths and widths. Do these different shapes remind you of square and rectangular objects in the world? Can you draw a cereal box? A locker? An aquarium? Also practice drawing your rectangle below and above the horizon line.

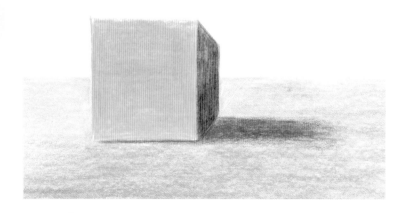

One-Point Perspective (Inside of a Box)

Tools Used: Pencil, Eraser, Colored Pencils, Ruler

NOW YOU'RE GOING TO DRAW AN INSIDE VIEW of a cube. Imagine you took the lid off a box and then turned it on its side so that the opening faces you. Drawing this inside view is important because it will help you draw rooms, bookshelves, and cubbies.

Step 1
Draw a horizon line across your page. Draw your vanishing point in the middle of that line. Draw a square just below the horizon. Then draw four straight lines connecting each of the square's four corners to the vanishing point.

Step 2
Draw the square that represents the back of the cube. The top and bottom lines should be parallel to the top and bottom lines of the front square. The sides of the back square should be parallel to the sides of the front square.

Step 3
Erase the perspective lines that extend behind the cube to the vanishing point.

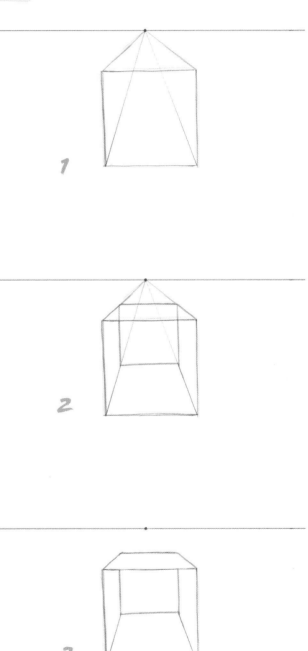

Step 4

Color the top of the cube a light color. Color the back of the cube a darker value of the same color.

Step 5

Color the inside walls and floor of the cube the same light-medium color that you used for the top.

Step 6

Using the darker value, darken the inside walls of the cube. Notice how a shadow is cast in a triangular shape toward the back of the side walls. As you shade the inside of the cube, think about how the areas that are farther away from the light (those areas farther back inside the cube) are going to be darker than the areas closer to the front, where the light source enters.

Step 7

Finally, use a contrasting color for the ground. I overlapped green and brown colored pencils to create this color.

On Your Own

Spend some time looking for one-point perspective in the world around you. Take the lid off a shoebox and turn it on its side so the opening faces you. Can you see how the four corners all angle in toward a vanishing point? Try drawing this. Now, zoom out and take a look at the room where you are right now. Position yourself so that you're facing a wall square on. Can you see how this room is just a big shoebox? If you're having a hard time seeing it, back up as far as you can. If you're still having a hard time seeing it, check out the room on the next page.

One-Point Perspective Room

Tools Used: Pencil, Eraser, Ruler, Markers

This room is basically the inside of a big, one-point perspective box. Pretty much everything in it is drawn using one-point perspective. Look on the next two pages to see some of the elements broken down into basic steps.

Here are the steps needed to
draw one of the chairs in the room.
Notice where the horizon line and
vanishing point are located.

1

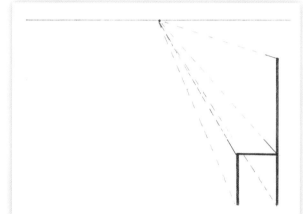

2

3

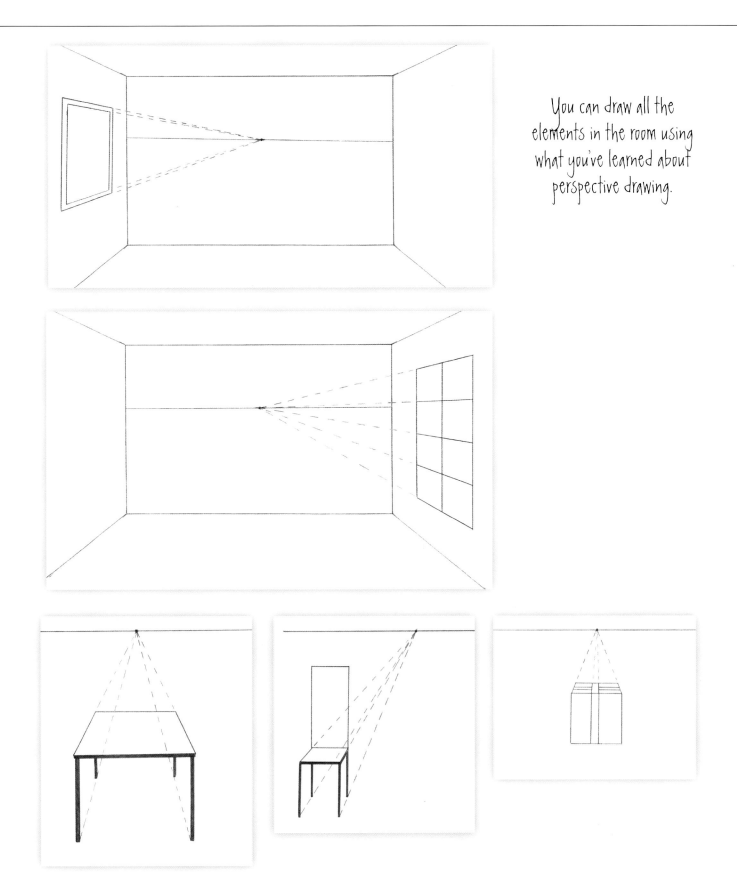

You can draw all the elements in the room using what you've learned about perspective drawing.

Two-Point Perspective Cube

Tools Used: Pencil, Eraser, Colored Pencils, Ruler

With two-point perspective, you have two vanishing points on the horizon line instead of one. So, instead of looking at something head-on like the square side of the cube on page 53, you're looking at its corner. Since you're looking at its edge, you can see two of the sides at once. This can be really cool if you want to draw a city block—you can look down two streets at the same time.

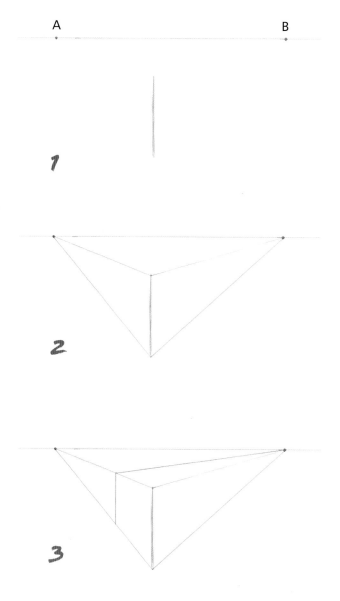

A   B

Step 1
Draw a horizon line across your page. Draw two vanishing points: one on each side of the page. Label these points point A (on the left) and point B (on the right). Between these two points, below the horizon line, draw a vertical line.

Step 2
Connect the top of the vertical line to each of the vanishing points. Connect the bottom of the vertical line to each of the vanishing points.

Step 3
Draw the back, vertical edge of your cube on the left side of the cube. This line should be parallel to the sides of your paper. Next, connect the top of this line, where it meets the perspective line, to point B.

Step 4

Draw the back, vertical edge of your cube on the right side of the cube. This line should be parallel to the sides of your paper. Next, connect the top of this line to point A.

Step 5

Erase all of the perspective lines that extend behind the cube. Now you have a very cool two-point perspective cube.

Step 6

Imagine where your light source is. I imagined mine was facing me to my left. I colored the top and left side of the cube a warm red. I colored the right side of the cube a darker, cool red.

Step 7

I cast a dark green shadow on the right, front side of the cube. See how the sides of the shadow connect back to vanishing point A? If you have trouble seeing it, take a ruler or your pencil and lay it flat on the book page. Use it to connect the sides of the shadows with vanishing point A. The front edge of the shadow lines up with vanishing point B. I colored the ground a bright, yellow-green. Because red and green are complimentary colors, the drawing has a lot of contrast and energy.

On Your Own

Try this the next time you're walking down the sidewalk near some buildings in a downtown area (this will be easier to see if you're somewhere that's pretty flat). Stop when you get to the street corner and turn around to face the corner of the building. You should be able to look down two streets at once. Can you see how it all lines up into two-point perspective? Can you visualize where the horizon line is in the distance? Try to approximate in your mind's eye where the vanishing points are.

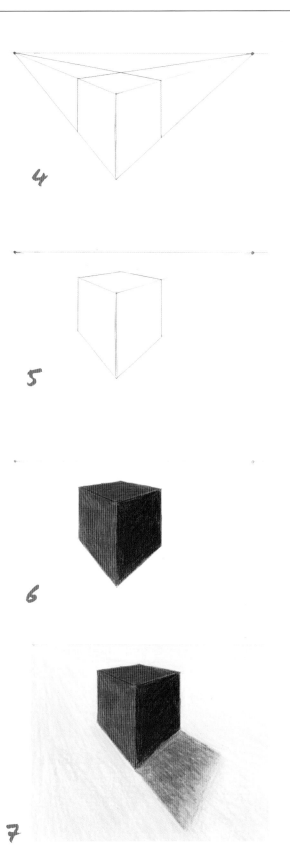

Chapter 6

DRAWING LANDSCAPES

Landscapes are great subjects for drawing with color. Since what you're drawing is far away, it keeps you from getting mired down in the detail of the drawing, and helps you focus on large, sweeping swaths of color. Next time you look out over a great vista, squint your eyes and try to identify the big areas of color. Sure, there may be thousands of colors that make up the view, but squinting can help you simplify what you see.

The rules of atmospheric perspective tell us that things appear lighter in color and fuzzier the farther away they are.

When you look up into the sky on a clear day, the blue is often brighter and more brilliant high in the sky.

In a cityscape the buildings in the foreground are more vibrant in color than the ones in the distance, which appear grayer.

Marker Mountain Range

I LIVE IN THE BLUE RIDGE MOUNTAINS, so when I go out hiking, this is the beautiful view I get to see! Remember how atmospheric perspective affects value; the mountains closest to us will be darker, but they will get progressively fuzzier and lighter the farther away from us they are.

Step 1
Use a light blue marker to draw a bumpy line of mountains across the page.

Step 2
Draw a second line of mountains below the first in a slightly darker color. You want to make sure to leave yourself plenty of room to go darker. You don't want to jump straight from your lightest blue to your darkest, or you won't leave yourself anywhere to go. Then, draw a third line of mountains below the second. Since I didn't have a lot of blue markers to choose from, I used the same marker as in the second set of mountains. I just drew over it a couple of times to make it darker.

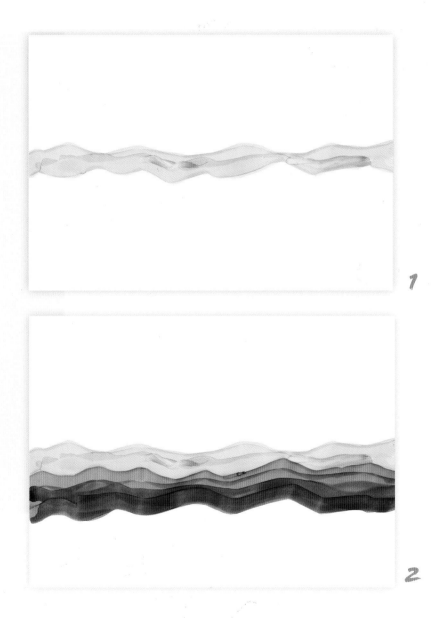

Step 3

I didn't really have a blue color dark enough for the fourth set of mountains. Color mixing to the rescue! I used a dark blue marker, colored over it with a green marker, and colored over it again with the blue. Experiment with layering different colors on scrap paper to see what combination you want to use. Using a light, sky blue color, draw the outlines of some big, fluffy clouds.

Step 4

Use the same marker to color in the blue sky around the clouds. If you have a couple of different light blue markers, you might want to play around with shifting the hue a little bit as it moves toward the horizon. Whenever you're outside, notice the color of the sky. It's constantly shifting hue and can be several different shades at once.

On Your Own

If you don't live near mountains, go outside and draw what you see! If the biggest expanse of land you see is your neighbor's front yard, draw that. Do you have a favorite tree in your neighborhood? That would make a great subject for a landscape drawing. If you live in the city, and you see more concrete than you do greenery, draw a cityscape! If you're in a high-rise building looking out over a big city, look to see if the rules of atmospheric perspective affect buildings the same way they do mountains.

Mountain Landscape

THIS MOUNTAIN RANGE is similar to the one you just drew. This time, you'll experiment with pastels, which are fun because, unlike markers, you can smear and smudge them to create soft edges. Remember, you don't have to use the same colors I use. Your mountains can be a spectrum of blues or greens or purples. The important thing is to get a range of values in your mountains.

Step 1
Sketch in the first mountain ridge. Usually, the closest mountains are the darkest. Use a lighter green to draw the next set of mountains.

Step 2

For the third set of mountains, use a medium blue color.

Step 3

For the farthest ridge overlap blue and white for a light, hazy color.

Step 4

Outline the clouds with a light gray pastel. Use a medium light blue for the sky above and around the clouds. Try using peach for the area of sky between the bottom of the clouds and the tops of the mountains.

Step 5

Use a gray pastel to add a layer of fluffy color to the clouds. Leave the top edges of the clouds white.

Step 6

Now go back over the whole drawing, darkening areas that need it. Sometimes I'll use a different color layered over the first to make a rich, dark tone. In the first set of mountains, for example, I layered dark blue over the green.

Step 7

Continue layering and defining. Add more dark gray to the clouds and more turquoise to define the edges of the tops of the clouds. Add a little purple to the bottoms of the clouds.

Step 8

Finally, add some gray to the peach area of sky. Continue to add a little bit of color here and there to make things pop. Don't overuse this technique. You don't need to outline everything.

On Your Own

When you go exploring for landscapes to draw, bring more than one type of drawing tool with you. Try drawing a landscape with colored pencils, and then, turn the page in your sketchbook and try it again with watercolor paints. I encourage you to experiment with different media as often as you can. You'll find that different materials have different qualities, and, as you play with them, you'll find what your favorites are. You'll also see that by drawing the same subject in a different medium, you will make a wildly different drawing.

Cloudscape

Tools Used: Pastels

YOU USUALLY CAN'T DRAW CLOUDS exactly as you see them because they are constantly changing. Instead, watch the clouds to see how they behave and move. Rely on your imagination, memory, and eyes to draw big, puffy clouds.

Step 1

After spending some time staring up at the sky, draw loose cloud shapes on your paper with a gray pastel. Resist the temptation to make "cloud" shapes—those are just symbols for clouds. Clouds rarely actually look like that. Instead, challenge yourself to draw the loose, blobby shapes that you see in the sky.

Step 2

Next, choose two different blues, one darker than the other. Use your darker blue to fill in the area around the clouds toward the top of your page. Use the lighter blue to fill in the area around the clouds toward the bottom.

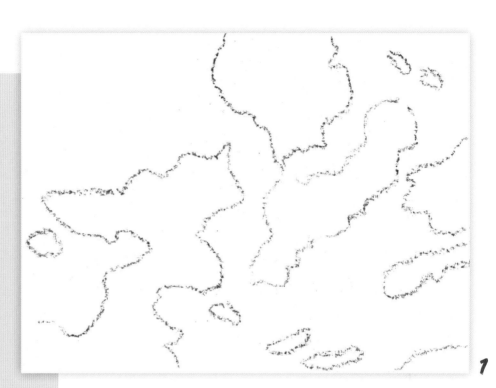

1

2

Step 3
Because you're drawing with pastels, you can use your finger to smudge the blue. See how soft the blues look once you blend them with your finger?

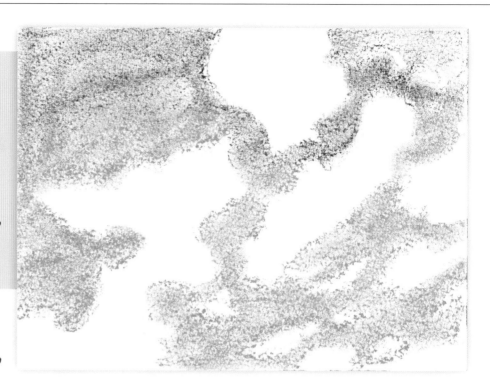

3

4

Step 4
Look up and see where the gray areas are on the clouds. Draw them in loosely with a gray pastel.

Step 5
Use a different finger (you don't want to smear blue into your clouds) to smudge the gray areas. They'll start to look soft and fluffy.

5

6

Step 6
To make your clouds "pop," use your blues to define small parts of the outlines of your clouds. I used a little bit of gray here and there to work back into the shadowy parts of the clouds.

On Your Own

Spend some time lying on your back staring at the clouds drifting across the sky. Any time spent carefully observing the world helps your drawing, even if you don't have a piece of paper or pencil anywhere in sight.

Ferris Wheel with Landscape

Tools Used: Colored Pencils, Markers

THE FERRIS WHEEL IS LOOKING PRETTY GOOD in Chapter 3 (page 38), but it's just hanging out on a plain white page. By adding sky, you'll ground the Ferris wheel and make the whole drawing feel more complete. More importantly, by adding color to the sky, you'll infuse the whole drawing with emotion and drama.

Step 1
I wasn't sure how bold I wanted the sky to be, so I started sketching in the lower part of the sky with a purple colored pencil. If you already know what you want to do, go for it.

Step 2
Outline small fluffy cloud shapes with a purple colored pencil. Leave the insides white and color the sky around them light blue.

Step 3
Experiment with some deep colors and use a marker to block in part of the sky.

Step 4

Keep adding color with the markers, and use deep purple for the lower part of the sky. Even though the sky didn't look like this when I drew the Ferris wheel, this is what the sky *felt* like to me. It was beautiful and dramatic and a little bit spooky.

Step 5

While I liked the new bold sky in my drawing, I noticed that some parts of the Ferris wheel were getting lost against it. I used some darker colors as well as bright red to add definition and make the Ferris wheel pop out. Take a step back from your drawing from time to time see what it needs.

Water Reflection Landscape

I LOVE THE WATER. It's so beautiful and mysterious, and swimming in it feels like flying. Drawing and painting water can be just as fun and magical. The water surface can act like a mirror. When the sun is just right, the water reflects whatever is above it.

Step 1

Saturate your brush with water and green paint and make a bold swash across the middle of your paper. Then, paint the fluffy bottoms of several clouds gray.

Step 2

Paint the sky bright blue. Start at the top of the page and work your way down. This makes the blue brighter at the top of the page, because your brush has more paint in it when you first start painting. Make sure to paint around the shapes of the clouds as you imagine them, leaving some white paper showing.

Step 3

Paint three leafless, winter trees with a dark color such as black. This creates a high contrast between the trees and their light-colored surroundings, making the trees look stark and dramatic. When you look at trees, notice how the branches get gradually skinnier as they grow away from the trunk. Pay attention to the way different trees grow. Some branches grow in graceful curves from their trunks, like beautiful arms reaching proudly to the sky. Other trees have jagged branches that zig and zag and grow at very sharp angles. Notice how the trunk flares slightly as it enters the ground and begins growing its strong, deep roots.

3

Step 4

Repeat the previous steps upside-down on the lower half of your paper. If it's easier for you, turn your paper upside-down first. Use a little more water in your brush because this is the surface of the pond, so things should look wetter. Don't worry about making a perfectly precise mirror image of what you've drawn. Just work quickly so the paint doesn't dry completely. Use a dry, clean brush to "paint" a few horizontal lines in the surface of the water. These little marks will look like ripples in the pond. You can see my marks most clearly in the reflection of the trees.

4

Chapter 7

DRAWING ANIMALS

THIS CHAPTER IS DIFFERENT BECAUSE, unlike blue tubes, boxes, or mugs, animals are animated! They're alive and have personalities and they move around. With the right use of color, you can bring their bodies to life. With a well-placed dot, you can add the twinkle to an animal's eye that makes her look like she's staring right back at you, as if she's got a clever thought on her mind. You can use color to create all kinds of different textures—from the waxed-papery wing of an insect to the loveable fuzziness of a kitten.

Dragonfly

Tools Used: Watercolor Pencils

I USED WATERCOLOR PENCILS for this drawing since they are especially good for making the wings look translucent. If you only have regular colored pencils, don't worry—your drawing will still look great.

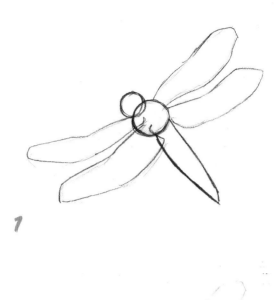

1

Step 1
Draw circles for the head and center body segment. For the tail, draw a long, thin shape that comes to a point at the end. Draw four petal-shaped wings.

Step 2
Lightly erase the pencil marks. This way, you can still see the shape of what you're drawing, but the pencil marks won't show through the color.

2

Step 3
Outline the wings with the background color of your choice and then sketch in the background.

3

Step 4

Dab the tip of your paintbrush in water and "paint" over your watercolor pencil lines. Don't worry about the background color bleeding into the wing shapes. A dragonfly's wing is sort of like a screen—you can see through it, but there are tiny little lines in it.

Step 5

Use a black pencil to fill in the head and center body and a purple pencil for the tail. I decided that the light source in my picture is coming from the upper right corner. So, the darkest side of the dragonfly's body is the one farthest away from the light source, the lower left. I left white paper exposed down the center of the body and tail for the highlight. Once you draw in your colors, paint them with the wet brush.

Step 6

Next, darken the top outline of the wings with a dark blue pencil. Draw some of the vein-like lines in the wings. Go over the lines with the wet brush.

Step 7

Continue to define the wings and add vein-like lines with brown and black pencils. Add spots of yellow in the outer tips of the wings.

On Your Own

Insects are interesting subjects to draw. The segments of their bodies are made up of pretty simple shapes. Since they're so fast and tiny, you may want to draw from a photograph to better observe all of the details up close. Or, the next time you see a dead bug on the windowsill, give it a pose and draw it.

Goldfish

Tools Used: Markers

SOMETIMES, IT'S MORE IMPORTANT TO CAPTURE THE MOVEMENT of an animal than to get every detail exactly right. A goldfish almost never slows down enough to be a still model for your drawing. When you're focusing on movement more than shape, you can toss out your pencil and dive right in with the color—incorporate any "mistakes" into your drawing. When drawing with markers, start with the lightest value and go darker with each step. This way, if you want to tighten up the drawing as you go, you can cover stray marks here and there with a darker color. Remember that with markers, you can always go darker but you can't go lighter.

Step 1

With a yellow marker, draw the overlapping oval shapes of the head and body. Don't worry about making neat, clean lines. Circle around and around with your marker until you have the shape you want. Then quickly shape up the chin area of the fish.

Step 2

Since the fish is swimming, its fins are moving and making loose, flowing shapes. Don't try to make these shapes perfect, because if the drawing gets too stiff, the fish won't look alive and in motion. Draw loose fins on the top, bottom, and sides of the fish's body, and add a long, flowing tail.

Step 3

With the same yellow marker, start to draw in the areas that are going to be the lightest. Leave some areas white so that the fish shimmers.

Step 4

With an orange marker, start to add color and definition to the face, the top of the head, and the back. Use the same orange markers to draw the stripy, vein-like lines in the fins. Notice the white space I left between the orange back and the yellow section of the fish's body. This is the highlight area that reflects the most light.

Step 5

Finally, choose a darker color for the shadow areas of the fish. (I used green, but you can try brown, dark orange, or even purple.) Darken under the chin and belly. Define the shadows around the fish's eye and gills. Overlap some orange areas of the fish's fins. Notice the area where the orange and green overlap, and mix a new color to add dimension to the drawing.

Kitty in Color

Tools Used: Colored Pencils

REMEMBER TIGER (PAGE 28)? Tiger's fuzzy looking coat is created with of a wide range of different shades of orange. I used a couple of different orange colored pencils. But, remember, if you only have one orange pencil, simply press down harder with the pencil for a darker value.

Step 1

Once you're happy with the general shape of Tiger (see pages 28 and 29), use an eraser to lighten up your lines. Draw the darkest stripes and patches of fur. Draw in quick, short marks in the direction that the kitten's fur grows. This way, as you add layers of color, you'll create a texture that looks like fur. Add and mix in another color such as brown to achieve a different hue. Think about texture as you're drawing. Imagine that each mark on Tiger's furry body is a single hair.

1

Step 2

Use an orange pencil to lightly sketch the base fur color on her back, legs, upper chest, and face. Keep her little muzzle, ears, and chest white for the moment. Color the insides of her ears, nose, and mouth with a rosy pink pencil. Try a peachy orange on her belly.

Step 3

Use an orange-brown color to darken the insides of her ears, the lines around her eyes, some of her stripes, and any other areas you think need a little definition. Define the right side of her nose and nostril with dark pink.

Step 4

Color her eyes light green, but leave the middle part white. Use gray and lavender to add shadow to her muzzle and chin and to add her little whisker dots. I used lavender because that's the color I saw in the shadow. You might see it differently. Sometimes I find using a color like lavender for a shadow, rather than just plain gray, can make the whole drawing more colorful and interesting. Since her whiskers are very light, just draw little dots on her muzzle from which her whiskers grow.

Step 5

Outline her green eyes and draw her pupils with dark blue. Leave a white shape in the middle of each pupil so that her eyes look bright and shiny. Add a little orange-brown to her eyes and some dark pink and purple for her mouth. Go over the whole drawing again with your oranges, adding layers of color to make her fur look soft.

On Your Own

You can use the skills you learned with Tiger to capture the texture of other fuzzy things. Do you have a fuzzy stuffed animal or pair of furry slippers that you'd like to draw? Notice things such as grass and the centers of some flowers that have a hair-like texture. Practice using your pencil marks to express the feel of fuzziness in your drawings.

Sadie

Tools Used: Colored Pencils

THIS IS MY DOG, SADIE. She's happy because she just played Frisbee and is now taking a rest in the grass while munching on a bone. Life just doesn't get any better than that. When people describe Sadie, they say she's a black and white dog, which is true. But it's also not true. Sadie is also brown and blonde and sometimes even a little blue in places.

Step 1
Draw three ovals for her head, upper body, and back hip. Draw ovals for the nose and lower jaw, front upper leg, and back hip. Draw ovals for the tops of the ears, eyes, knees, and paws.

Step 2

Connect the back hip and chest ovals by drawing a nice, long curve for the back, and another for the curve of the belly. Connect the ear ovals to the head to make perky triangular ears. Draw the front legs. Connect the head oval with the chest oval with a little "C" shaped curve in the neck area. Draw the nose. It's almost (but not quite) heart-shaped. Draw the shape of her open mouth.

Step 3

Clean up the drawing a bit and erase all of the guide ovals. Draw the little rectangular bone between her paws.

Step 4

Sketch in the reddish browns and yellows in her undercoat that show through the black fur on her shoulder, neck, face, and head. Draw short, quick lines in the same direction that her fur grows.

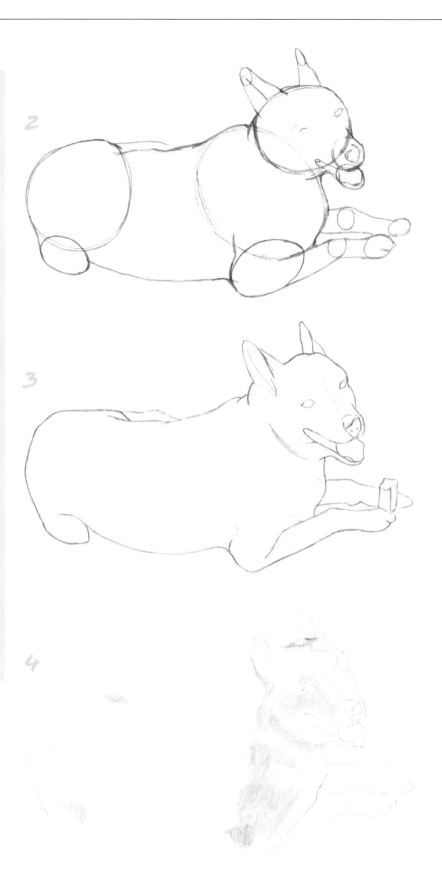

Step 5

Highlight the areas on the middle and top of her back with a light blue pencil. I could have just used white for these areas, but sometimes Sadie's coat is so shiny black that it almost looks blue. Using blue instead of white will give you a richer drawing.

Step 6

Start adding the dark browns to her shoulder, neck, and body. Notice how I pressed harder in some areas, like the fronts of her legs, to get a darker value. Add gray to her neck, nose, ears, and the top of her head.

Step 7

Finish drawing Sadie's fur with her main color—black. Draw in the direction that her fur grows. Overlap and draw over the brown and blue areas of her undercoat. When you're adding black to her head and face, make sure to leave the blaze going down her nose white.

Step 8

Use pink for the tongue and grayish lavender for the shadow of the tongue. Draw the irises (the colored part) of her eyes with a light brown center and dark brown outline. Use black to draw her pupils and outline her eyes. With the reddish brown pencil, go back over the light areas of her face, ears, and shoulders. Color the bone with a tan pencil, adding a dark red center.

Step 9

Use several different colors of green and yellow to scribble in the grass with quick, loose marks. See how the yellow sections of grass make it appear like the sun is filtering through the trees?

Chapter 8

DRAWING PEOPLE

Now, ALL OF THOSE TUBES AND EGGS you drew are going to come in handy. People are the most amazing subjects to draw. Human faces and bodies are so expressive; they are capable of communicating so much by raising an eyebrow or kicking a foot. As complex as they are, people can be drawn using the same basic shapes and lines. You just have to practice seeing the simple shapes inside these complicated forms.

Faces Are Hard (Boiled)

PEOPLE OFTEN TELL ME THAT FACES ARE DIFFICULT to draw. But, if you can draw an egg and parentheses (the little C-shaped things around these words), then you can draw a simple face.

Step 1

Draw an egg shape like the one on page 36. This time, however, pretend you can magically stand your egg on its small, pointed end. Notice how the light source is coming from the left side and the shadow is on the right side.

Step 2

Draw a line through the center of the egg. You might want to measure with a ruler to make sure the line is right in the middle of the egg, dividing the top and bottom in perfect halves. Or, rather than drawing a line straight across the egg that you will have to erase later, just make two little marks, one on either side of the egg, to guide your eye to the center of the egg. Now, in the centerline of the egg, draw two parenthesis shapes for the closed eyes. Below those shapes, draw two more parenthesis shapes for the sides of the nose.

Step 3

Between the sides of the nose, draw an upturned parenthesis. Below the nose draw four little parentheses for the upper lip. The two in the center are the top and bottom lines of the upper lip. The ones on the sides are the corners of the mouth.

Step 4

Connect the center parentheses to the corners of the mouth. Add a bigger parenthesis to mark the bottom of the lower lip. Add a smaller, upside-down parenthesis for the shadow of the chin beneath the lower lip. Add two little parentheses to define the bridge of the nose between the eyes; notice how they turn outward a little. Draw two, tiny upside down parentheses for the nostrils. Add two, wide upside-down parentheses for the eyebrows. Now you have a good-looking face—with nothing more than an egg and a few parentheses.

Step 5

I've drawn some lines over my hard-boiled egg-face to show you a little bit about proportion—where features are supposed to go on the face in relation to everything else. The solid horizontal line in the middle of the face is the eye line. When people are first learning to draw faces, it is very common for them to put the eyes too high on the face, where the forehead should go. Your eyes are actually in the middle of your head! Go look in the mirror and check for yourself. Your eyes might try to play tricks on you—but don't just measure to your hairline—measure to the top of your head. Another fun way to check proportion is with a photo in a magazine of a person looking straight ahead (if her head is tilted up or down, this won't work). Use a ruler and measure.

On Your Own

Not only have you just drawn a great egg-head face, but you've also plotted out all the important points of the "face map." All of those guidelines will help when you're drawing faces. Practice drawing the face map without looking at this page.

4

5

The eye line is five eyes across.

The nose is usually a little shorter than the halfway mark between the eye line and the chin.

If you have trouble figuring out the size and placement of the ears, just draw a little line marking where the eyebrows go and the bottom of the nose goes. The ears should fit right between these lines!

Facial Features

NOW THAT YOU'VE LEARNED HOW TO DRAW a simple face, it's time to explore the features of the face a little further. Think about what you learned about shape and shadow when you drew the orange on page 34. By thinking about these facial features as spheres or ovals, you can add light and shadow and give them a sense of volume and three-dimensionality. Practice drawing eyes, ears, mouths, and noses in greater detail.

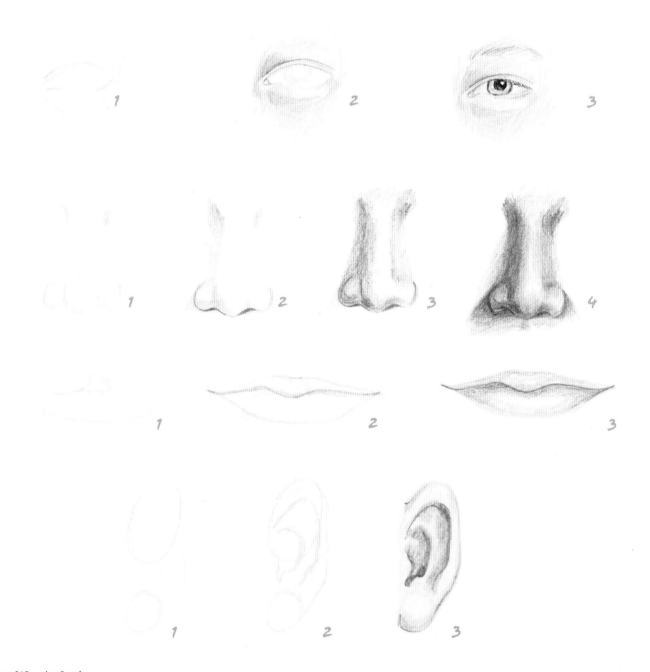

Girl's Face

Tools Used: Pencil, Eraser, Colored Pencils

WHEN YOU'RE STARTING OUT DRAWING FACES, it's important not to get too worried about making them look just like the people you're drawing. Instead, focus on finding shapes, seeing shadows, and using the person or picture as a point of reference. There's so much to find and see in the human face in terms of color. Human skin comes in a beautiful range of colors and tones. There's so much variety and so much personality: warm browns, cool pinks, golden tans, freckly peaches with blue undertones, and every conceivable tone in between!

Step 1

Draw an ellipse for her face. Sketch in the major face-map guidelines you learned on the egg-face on page 91. Draw circles for her eyes, cheekbones, nose, chin, mouth, and ear. Sketch in hair and eyebrows. Further sharpen any important details, and erase the guidelines.

Step 2

Gently rub your eraser over your drawing, softening your pencil lines. Use a cool, dark brown pencil (I used sepia) to lightly sketch in the mid-tone shadows.

Step 3

Strengthen the darker shadows. Pay special attention to the folds of her cheeks, her nostrils, the corners of her smile, her eyelids, and the darkest areas in her hair. Then, sketch in the pink areas, overlapping the pink color with the sepia mid-tones you've already drawn. Make sure to leave some areas white for the highlights.

Step 4

Sketch in the peach colored areas. This is the predominant color in her face. Make sure to overlap this color into the shadow areas. Press more firmly in the darker, shadowy areas, and more lightly in the highlight areas. Again, remember to leave a few highlight spots white—like on her left cheek and the tip of her nose.

Step 5

Because her upper lip is slightly in shadow, it's a darker, more purple-pink than the lower lip. I chose a lavender color for the upper lip and for the shadow areas of her lower lip. I used a warm pink for the rest of the lower lip. Use a light neutral color, such as gray, for the teeth. If you outline the teeth too darkly, they will look like big, clunky, horse teeth. Instead, focus on the bottom shapes of the teeth. See how each tooth is a little rounded on the edge as it meets the next tooth. Very lightly draw the lines between each tooth. Use a dark gray to draw in the shadowy area beneath her top teeth.

4

5

Step 6

Block in the highlight areas of the hair—she has some reddish highlights on the left side of her part, and yellowish ones on the right. Sketch in the mid-brown tones. Darken the dark areas. You may want to use a black colored pencil for the darkest areas in the hair. Remember, as with the cat on page 82, you can create texture by paying attention to your marks. Make sure your lines "grow" in the same direction that the hair grows.

Step 7

Add your final details. Darken the pupils and the area around the iris, being careful to leave dots of white, which are highlights that make her eyes sparkle. Darken areas that you may have blocked in lightly earlier, such as her eyebrows and the corners of her mouth. Give the whole drawing a final sweep with your peach, pink, and brown pencils to add richness to her skin tone. Use a different, warmer brown pencil (if you have one) to add more dimension to the shadows.

Boy's Face

Tools Used: Pencil, Eraser, Colored Pencils

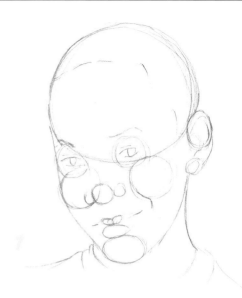

THIS MODEL HAS A BEAUTIFUL RANGE OF TONES IN HIS SKIN, from warm peach to a cool, dark brown. Though I only used a handful of colored pencils for this drawing, I varied my pressure and layered the colors to create a range of values and hues.

Step 1
Draw the basic shapes of the face: the brain and chin circles, the cheeks, the eyes, the three circles for the nose, the lips, and the two ovals for the ear.

Step 2
After shaping up the face and erasing the guidelines, lightly erase the whole pencil drawing. Next, begin by blocking in the light warm peach color. Focus on the parts of his face receiving the most light, like the nose, the cheeks, and the forehead. Also block in the peach in areas that will later mostly be in shadow, like the sides of his cheekbones. The warmth of the peach will show through the layers of color you apply later. Make sure to leave a few highlight areas white.

Step 3
Use a medium brown pencil (I used a color called sienna) to begin sketching in some mid-tones. Notice how I drew lightly to create some of the mid-tones and bore down harder to create some of the darker areas, like the inside curve of his ear, the sides of his nose, and parts of his neck. Use a purple-pink color on his lips. His top lip is more in shadow and is a little darker. Leave a highlight area white in the middle of his lower lip.

Step 4

Use your brown color to deepen the mid-tones and shadows even further. Go back over the highlight areas and mid-tones with the peach color to add warmth.

Step 5

Sketch in the hair with a black pencil. Notice how his hair is darker and thicker toward the back of his head and thinner toward the hairline. His hair is curly and cropped very short, so make many little sketchy marks to recreate his hair texture. Draw the eyebrows, the pupils, and eyelashes. Use a darker brown to deepen the shadow areas in his face.

Step 6

Go back over the face with the peach and sienna colors to deepen his skin tone and make it look more saturated and rich. Use a gray pencil to add shadows to the whites of his eyes. Notice how the corners and the area just under the upper lid are in shadow. Use the same gray pencil to add subtle shadows to his shirt. Use pink and lavender pencils to add richness to his lip color.

Tubes & Spheres = Bodies

Building a body out of oranges and toilet paper rolls

REMEMBER WHEN WE DREW THE ORANGE AND THE BLUE TUBE in Chapter 3? By practicing simple shapes, you've prepared yourself to draw something as complex as the human body. Like everything that's complicated, it helps to break your drawing down into sections and simple shapes. When you're drawing the human figure, imagine each segment of the body as a tube and each joint as a sphere. Take a look at the two figures below. Notice how the tubes and spheres move into different positions and angles as the body moves.

Draw a Body

Tools: Pencil, Eraser

Try drawing this basic figure, and then practice drawing different types of
bodies by changing the sizes and shapes of your tubes and spheres.

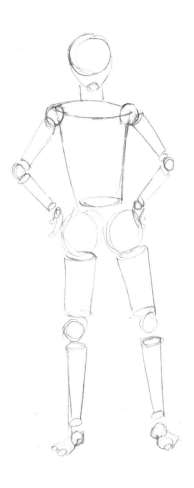

Step 1
Draw a sphere for the part of the skull that contains the brain. Draw
a short, medium-width tube for the neck, and a wider tube for the
torso. Draw spheres for the shoulders, thin tubes for the upper arm
bones, spheres for the elbows, and tubes for the forearms. Draw
larger spheres for the hip sockets and continue in the same fash-
ion—tubes for the thigh bones, spheres for the knees, tubes for the
shin bones, and so on.

Step 2
Round out the lines by imagining the bulges of muscle and
fat on this basic "skeleton." Draw the skin that makes this
body look organic and human. Imagine the light source, and
using what you know about how light falls over spheres and
tubes, shade your figure.

Dancer

THE IMPORTANT THING WITH A DRAWING like this is to capture the feeling of the moving body. Your drawing gestures should be quick and free, just like the movements of the dancer. Getting all the fingers, toes, eyes, and ears right where they "should" be doesn't matter at all. Don't allow yourself to get hung up on perfection—that will just dull your artistic spirit and dampen the energy in the drawing.

Step 1
Use a light purple wash and just a few brush-strokes to sketch in the basic shape. Don't worry about making the shape perfect. This should be fun; enjoy the movement of the brush across the page.

1

Step 2

Use dark teal-blue and dark purple to sketch in the shadows in the folds of the dancer's hoodie and jeans. To make dark brush strokes you need more paint and only a little water on the brush.

Step 3

Add a few strokes of a warm, tan color for the arms and face. Don't worry about painting facial features or all of the individual fingers. The movement is what matters here, not the details. Make a few dark gray marks for the soles and laces of the shoes.

On Your Own

Next time you're at the park, a dance recital, or a soccer game—anytime you're watching people in motion—pay extra attention to the ways their bodies move. Notice how the kicker leans forward as she runs, how the dancer arches his back as he leaps, and how the kid on the swing leans his head back and flexes his feet, stretching his legs toward the sky. Then, allow yourself two minutes, and only a few strokes of the brush or the pencil to capture the movement. Ignore detail. Let your marks play on the page the way that person is traveling across the field or the stage.

Girls with Kite

IN THE PAST CHAPTERS YOU'VE DRAWN PLACES, LANDSCAPES, AND ROOMS. Now, draw a setting and let your figures play there. Keep your marks loose and rhythmic to match the energy of the girls and their colorful kite. If you feel like throwing caution to the wind, dive right in with your markers!

Step 1

Sketch out the basic shape of the figures using circles for the joints and tubes for the torso and segments of arms and legs.

Step 2

Sketch the clothing and the kite. Can you see how the kite is essentially made up of two triangles that are touching at their bases? Draw the hair and the tail ribbons of the kite.

Step 3
Sketch in the grassy horizon. Continue to add detail to the figures and the kite. The light source is coming from the upper left corner. Go ahead and lightly sketch some shadows on the girls' shirts, shorts, and bodies.

Step 4
Lightly erase your pencil lines so that they're still visible, but won't dull the colors of the marker. Begin blocking in one color for each major area, making sure you have a light and darker tone of each color you plan to use. Start with the lighter color. For the shirt of the girl on the left, for example, I used a bright, clear pink—the color for the highlight and mid-tones of the shirt. You'll use the darker color in the next step. Since I didn't have a peach colored marker, I used colored pencil for the girls' skin. Add color to the kite.

Step 5

Remember that the brightest light source is coming from the upper left. Therefore, the darkest shadow areas are on the right sides of the figures, the areas farthest away from the light source. Notice the shadows under their arms and how the subtle but important shadows on the kite make it look like sunlight is shining through the fabric. See how the shirt on the right casts a shadow on the top of her blue shorts. Using the darker colors you set aside earlier, add shadows to each area of your drawing.

Step 6

Create a bright blue sky and a thick field of grass. I used two different colors of blue marker for my sky and thick, curving lines to create a sense of movement and play. For the grass, I used three different colors of green. I colored the whole area with one color with wide, horizontal lines. Then I made lots of quick, short vertical marks. The color still wasn't as dense as I wanted it to be, so I scribbled wildly. Just for fun, I made some random, abstract marks like little "x" shapes and a few rectangular shapes with the fat side of my marker. I kept making lots of marks until the grass looked as lush and layered as I wanted it.

On Your Own

Practice drawing people in settings: standing in the kitchen, pouring a glass of orange juice, or sitting on the bench waiting for a bus. Remember, you can give them a real sense of "being there" by paying attention to light and shadow. Find your light source and cast a shadow on the floor or the sidewalk on the opposite side.

COLOR YOUR IMAGINATION

HAVE YOU EVER BEEN DRAWING OR daydreaming when, out of nowhere, an idea or an image pops into your head? Perhaps something you haven't thought about or seen quite that way before? The imagination is a mysterious thing. It's like the soil or the ocean. It's deep and dark and there is so much life in it. It's filled with images and ideas that no one but you will put together. So, anytime you feel that spark, listen very closely. It's a messenger from your imagination, delivering a new thought, a new image.

The drawing skills you've learned in this book should never be the main focus of your drawing. Instead, they should serve your imagination. Let your imagination take charge, and use the techniques and tools to multiply the possibilities of what you can create on your page.

On a Tightrope

Chapter 9: Color Your Imagination

IN THIS DRAWING, I IMAGINED A GIRL WEARING A CROWN of ribbons and green spheres, walking across the night sky on a tightrope suspended by the sheer power of her imagination. I painted the sky a royal purpley blue and painted the clouds grayish lavender. I imagined a skirt made of orange cone shapes. I used the same basic shading technique we used for the blue tube on page 32. This time, I just gave the tubes irregular base shapes and drew them so they came to a point, gathering together at her waist. After the watercolor dried, I used a red colored pencil to draw the tightrope string.

Fishscape

I USED PERSPECTIVE AND SHADING TECHNIQUES to make a funky strange interior where bubbles burble and goldfish swish in and out of blue columns.

Drawing Bubbles

Aren't these bubbles great? They're so much easier to draw than you'd think. Since bubbles are mostly clear, most of the color comes from what we see through their transparent surface. First, draw your whole drawing in marker. Then, collect lids and jars in a wide variety of sizes out of the kitchen cabinets. Trace different size circles onto your drawing with a colored pencil. Overlap some and leave others floating by themselves. Since, in this drawing, I imagined my light source coming from the upper right, I bore down hard with my white colored pencil on the upper right side of my bubbles to create a highlight. I then used my white pencil a little more lightly to draw a white curved shape on the left and lower right inside edges of the bubble. Notice how I left a little of the background between the outside edge of the bubble and this curved white area. Randomly in the middle of the bubble, I drew lightly with my white pencil to create milky, blurry areas. I used colored pencils that more-or-less matched the marker colors of the background to make a few edges and areas pop.

Acknowledgments

I would like to thank Betty Edwards and Mona Brooks for their inspiring work.

Enormous thanks are due to the talented people who made this book a reality. Thanks to Rain Newcomb, for her many, many long hours of work, brainstorming this book into being, sculpting it into an actual shape, and for making all of those many work meetings feel like play. Thanks to Joe Rhatigan, a great guy to work with and an incredibly gifted children's book editor, for all of his work bringing everything together and crafting this book into its final form. I so enjoyed working together again. Many thanks to Celia Naranjo, for her extraordinary design talent and her knack for making everything so much more beautiful than I ever could have imagined.

Thanks to Lyme for everything.

Thanks to Mom and Dad for their unbelievably abundant support and encouragement.

Thanks to Will, Claire, and all of my dear friends who inspire me and keep me playful and childish in the best of ways.

Eternal gratitude to my dear friend John Payne, who I miss terribly. He understood that art and play go together like peanut butter and chocolate.

Index

OKANAGAN REGIONAL LIBRARY
3 3132 02974 3897